BOA
EDITIONS LTD

T0161085

CAW

Books by Michael Waters

Caw 2020
The Dean of Discipline 2018
Celestial Joyride 2016
Selected Poems (UK) 2011
Gospel Night 2011
Darling Vulgarity 2006
Parthenopi: New and Selected Poems 2001
Green Ash, Red Maple, Black Gum 1997
Bountiful 1992
The Burden Lifters 1989
Anniversary of the Air 1985
Not Just Any Death 1979
Fish Light 1975

Editor:

Border Lines: Poems of Migration (with Mihaela Moscaliuc) 2020
Reel Verse: Poems About the Movies (with Harold Schechter) 2019
Contemporary American Poetry (with A. Poulin, Jr.) Eighth Edition,
    2006; Seventh Edition, 2001
Perfect in Their Art: Poems on Boxing from Homer to Ali (with Robert
    Hedin) 2003
A. Poulin, Jr. Selected Poems 2001
Dissolve to Island: On the Poetry of John Logan 1984

CAW

poems by

Michael Waters

American Poets Continuum Series, No. 181

BOA Editions, Ltd. ● Rochester, NY ● 2020

First Edition
20 21 22 23 7 6 5 4 3 2 1

For information about permission to reuse any material from this book, please contact
The Permissions Company at www.permissionscompany.com or e-mail permdude@
gmail.com.

Publications by BOA Editions, Ltd.—a not-for-profit corporation under NATIONAL
section 501 (c) (3) of the United States Internal Revenue Code—are made ENDOWMENT
possible with funds from a variety of sources, including public funds from ≡ARTS
the Literature Program of the National Endowment for the Arts; the New arts.gov
York State Council on the Arts, a state agency; and the County of Monroe,
NY. Private funding sources include the Max and Marian Farash Charitable
Foundation; the Mary S. Mulligan Charitable Trust; the Rochester Area
Community Foundation; the Ames-Amzalak Memorial Trust in memory
of Henry Ames, Semon Amzalak, and Dan Amzalak; the LGBT Fund of
Greater Rochester; and contributions from many individuals nationwide. See Colophon
on page 96 for special individual acknowledgments.

Cover Design: Daphne Morrissey
Cover Art: René Magritte, "Les Fanatiques (The Fanatics)," 1945. Image copyright
    © 2019 C. Herscovici / Artists Rights Society (ARS), New York
Interior Design and Composition: Richard Foerster
BOA Logo: Mirko

BOA Editions books are available electronically through BookShare, an online distributor
offering Large-Print, Braille, Multimedia Audio Book, and Dyslexic formats, as well as
through e-readers that feature text to speech capabilities.

Library of Congress Cataloging-in-Publication Data

Names: Waters, Michael, 1949– author.
Title: Caw : poems / by Michael Waters.
Description: First Edition. | Rochester, NY : BOA Editions, Ltd., 2020. |
    Series: American poets continuum series ; no. 181 | Summary: "Waters's 13th collection
    delves into aging, caretaking, the shifting landscape of modern marriage, and the
    slippery nature of familial memory"— Provided by publisher.
Identifiers: LCCN 2020003038 (print) | LCCN 2020003039 (ebook) | ISBN
    9781950774128 (paperback) | ISBN 9781950774135 (ebook)
Subjects: LCGFT: Poetry.
Classification: LCC PS3573.A818 C39 2020 (print) | LCC PS3573.A818
    (ebook) | DDC 811/.54—dc23
LC record available at https://lccn.loc.gov/2020003038
LC ebook record available at https://lccn.loc.gov/2020003039

BOA Editions, Ltd.
250 North Goodman Street, Suite 306
Rochester, NY 14607
www.boaeditions.org
A. Poulin, Jr., Founder (1938–1996)

CONTENTS

for

Mihaela

Kiernan

Fabian

this human chain

Mother of flames
You have kept the fire burning!
　　　　—William Carlos Williams

Lord Lord Lord caw caw caw Lord Lord Lord caw caw caw Lord
　　　　—Allen Ginsberg

CAW

SELF-PORTRAIT WITH DOLL (1920–21)

I have come to hate myself
As Kokoschka despised his doll,
Life-sized, red-haired, perfect in every part,
Horsehair and feathers
Sewn into the image of Alma Mahler
Who'd left him during the war,
But with whom he now slept
As she mouthed in dreams
His scars, gunshot and bayonet,
Until one night in drunken stupor
He forced himself to murder
His mute, immobile lover.
His fantasy was flawed,
And I have come to hate myself
For loving you so imperfectly, for craving
Your body, its clefts and moist creases,
Perfumes and spices,
And all the positions your limbs assume
During lovemaking.
                         I apologize
For this inexhaustible desire
For your lashes and lobes, the vertical
Slash of your navel,
The light strobing the hollow
At the base of your spine . . .
And for your breath, always your breath
Which keeps us both alive.

SWYVE

"If that I may, yon wenche wil I swyve."
—Chaucer, "The Reeve's Tale"

Take *apple*, for example, exhalation
Then expulsion, swoon then pow,
Old English *æpple* of Germanic origin,
The word released from the lips
So appealingly—that weary pun—

Or *swivel*, the pleasure of the pelvis
In its beckoning gyration, cool hula,
Derived from the Middle English
Swīfan, "to move," "to revolve," whence
The vulgar Chaucerian verb.

In Romanian, *Ce faci?* asks "How are you?"
And the civil response is *Fac bine*—
Loosely pronounced "fuck beanie"—
Meaning I'm doing well, *fac*
A declension of "to do" or "to make," so

My daughter, twelve, learning the language,
Would wisecrack, "Hey, let's *fac* a cake!"
Don't we all try to get away
With a few mild transgressions,
Words and hips given us to swivel

To our own purposes, mostly innocent
Though sometimes not, as when Eve,
Freshly alive, offered that creature
Who hadn't yet spoken her once-bitten
Apple as invitation: to taste, to *aah!* and to swyve.

DEAREST CREATURE

Middlebury Octopus Lab

An octopus the size of a fist
Fell in love with a marine biologist,
Teasing her philtrum with the tip
Of a tentacle when cupped

Near her amused & curious face,
Curling another around one ear,
Probing her lips with a timid third.
The rest encircled her left hand,

Stroking the brilliant wedding band.
Giddy with pleasure, the creature
Flashed colors like a living gem
Before the long unfastening.

That octopus one night unscrewed
The steel star-punched lid of its tank
To comb the corridors of the lab.
When in the morning she found that rag

She wept at love's barbed lure. How far
We urge ourselves to travel
To nuzzle a breast, tongue a navel,
Or fondle even a wisp of fur

Below the belly of a lover.

PILETA CAVE

Paleolithic art

bearded goat   vulva   pregnant mare
deer   bison   fish   vulva
bull   vulva   man with spear

which to worship   which to fear

GOOD RIDDANCE CHICKEN

My wife still cooks some meals
Using my ex-girlfriend's recipes,
Their familiar cursive once thrilling
In those years of exchanging letters
With their catalogs of arousal, divulging
Where we would taste each other
On those weekends we managed to erase
The distance between her home and mine.
Maryland-Connecticut. I-95. Driving
Through downpour or snow, blasting
Cranberries or Counting Crows.
She prepared exquisite meals,
Artichoke Heart Soufflé or
Bass Fillets Poached with Fennel
For my midnight arrival,
Coddled Eggs with Shallots
For breakfast, then mailed the recipes
So that I might in her absence recreate
Each savory morsel.
                    Now my wife
Revises each directive, shunning
Grapes but adding orange wheels
Or switching shiitake for wild chanterelle,
Purring with Rihanna on the radio,
Crossing out the name of each dish
At the top of the creased index card
To substitute one of her own invention,
But growing quiet when she reads, again,
Looped at the bottom of her favorite recipe,
The one for Chilled Roquefort Chicken,
"Always better when you add my company."

SPELLING LESSON

When we flatlined she left behind
Miles Davis' *In a Silent Way.*

As I listened to the exquisite
Undersea cries of the trumpet

Drawn from depths
Where words do not exist,

I wasn't sure which one of us
Was more relieved to be apart—

Then realized I'd never learned
The proper spelling of her name,

T-r-a-c-y or T-r-a-c-i,
That last *i* dotted with a heart.

SCIENTIFIC AMERICAN

Who knows where in the body love resides,
But it's not the heart, all muscle & always
Intent on its labor . . . more likely
Love bobs below our bellies
In ruptures & fissures
That sometimes shudder
Their roiling waters into the minor
Ocean of blood & bile,
As long ago they rumbled in pitch-black
Unfathomable depths where,
By light of their own making,
Curious creatures located each other
To continue their kind, not love exactly. . . .

Those almost invisible
Gob-like jellies of ebb & flow
& flickering glow
Remind us of what we might be
If stripped of our bodies
And what we were before
The unimaginably slow
Rapture when breathers began to assume
Flesh, sprout limbs, walk upright, even
Invent language until one day
Some creature that looks like me
Could write this poem
For some creature that looks like you.

VS.

When I thought I might lose my two-year-old
To the machinations of her mother,
I lay awake, the lent mattress muffling
My tom-toming heart & warped floorboards
In an empty (so spooky) railroad flat,
The adamant moon slashing reproaches
Through barred windows, the obscenities—
Ten thousand thousand fox-barked fuck yous—
Not in my runaway brain but echoed
From the Wells Fargo ATM drive-through
Where rowdy skaters kickflipped boards.
How easy to feel sorry for myself.
The solitary piece of furniture,
An airy four-poster canopy bed,
Cocooned my daughter in the next room,
Her sleep-sighs loud enough for me to love.
Then pain lightning'd through one finger—
I flailed it off & darkness tore away
To wedge itself into night's hellish niche
Before I could leap up to flick the switch.
Two pinpricks welled blood on my fingertip.
I woke my daughter to inspect each inch
Of rosy unblemished toddler flesh,
Then let her lullaby herself till dawn,
Waffles & juice, the goodbye at pre-K
Where her mother—*her* day—would retrieve her.
In Urgent Care an hour after coffee,
The stumped doctor texted the shelter's vet
Who viewed the punctures & pronounced them *bat*.
I'd have to flush the creature out
Or suffer the series of rabies shots.

No luck at home despite such lack—
Nooks hid nothing but spiders & crud.
So while lawyers jockeyed & my daughter
Shuttled between her mad keepers,
The first dose tunneled into the wound,
That needle longer than my now thrice-pierced
Finger. You must have heard me scream & thought
A rocket shattered sound across plumed skies.
Inside my body serum fought virus
(If rabies truly had invaded me)
Like radiated monsters from sea depths
In post-WWII Japanese flicks.
Several more shots mined salt from my eyes.
When all the dragged-out battles ceased, I glimpsed
The future:
               my body cleansed of toxins,
& equal time with my girl, the heart's needle,
For whom, to celebrate, I bought a doll
Who wept real tears & wet herself silly
& began to counsel me on joy.

for Kiernan

BOHEMIANS

"Whitman's preferred trousers through the late 1850s were 'bloomers,' the loose-fitting pants that were the male equivalent of those worn by women's rights activists."

—Karen Karbiener, "Introduction," *Leaves of Grass*

Walt Whitman sporting bloomers
Tucked inside leather boots
Quaffs dark German ale in Pfaff's,
Holding court for his "darlings and gossips"—
One hundred years before Stonewall,
Where he would have knuckled cops.

Now vendors assault each other
Over curb-space for carts before lunch hour:
Doner kebab, shawarma, spicy noodle
Eeling through broth, simmering.
Summer in the city. Immigrant odors
Quicken the lower reaches of heaven.

Walt steps off the ferry to hurry uptown,
Past wagons hauled by horses
Upon whom he rehearses pet names
Sugar   Ruffian   Eager   Kissin' Cousin
For the boys who, wearing the red trousers
Of the 14th Regiment New York State Militia,

Will be killed in the First Battle of Bull Run.

SHERRY

in memoriam JJ

Andalusian aperitif.
Color = straw = cream = amber.
Amontillado Oloroso Manzanilla
& Fino our prof professed to adore
As wide-eyed around him we yoga'd the floor,
Office walls postered with vintage signage
Foraged in Jerez de la Frontera.
Pouring with an operatic gesture
Like a semi-pro venenciador,
A whip of wine snapped from his sure hand,
He quarter-filled our Solo cups once more,
Then asked me to read aloud some "juicy"
Dialogue from *'Tis Pity She's a Whore*:
Italian incest in Brit tragedy.
Our seminar starred coed twins
At whom we'd glance aroused & askance.
Anything seemed possible in this class.
Then suddenly our Europhile died,
Askew in his office (spring break, suicide).
How many empty bottles of sherry?
Our palates opened to subtleties of age,
He broadened now our knowledge of pity.

ONE LAST BEAT

Wheelchair'd, catheter'd,
Mini prongs clasping septum,
The oxygen cylinder
A clunky steampunk accessory,
He dry-lipped a joint,
Dewar's sloshing over
The jiggling City Lights coffee mug,
Ice clinking, always clinking
(I can hear it now), & whispered a poem.
Who resembled in his diminishing
A seam-split straw doll,
Who siphoned words from a well
Still fountaining in the keening
Catacombs of the body.
Outside the window, his husband
Gardened, fingernails raking soil,
Planting gentian, hyacinth, & larkspur,
The three shades of grief for the one
Who turned away, gazed down
At each cube releasing invisibly
Its singular clarity into the amber
Swirl.
      "Can I get you anything?"
"Yes," he rasped, quoting Ferlinghetti,
"A rebirth of wonder."

mother of flames

for my mother
b. 1927

A small picture presented the interior of an immensely long and rectangular vault or tunnel, with low walls, smooth, white, and without interruption or device. Certain accessory points of the design served well to convey the idea that this excavation lay at an exceeding depth below the surface of the earth. No outlet was observed in any portion of its vast extent, and no torch or other artificial source of light was discernible; yet a flood of intense rays rolled throughout, and bathed the whole in a ghastly and inappropriate splendor.

—Edgar Allan Poe, "The Fall of the House of Usher"

the book of names

---

dead lovers of our fathers   possessors
of the once common but then abandoned
names—
        Edith   Gladys   Theodora   Pearl
khaki-wackies   leotarded hipsters—
names given over to modest markers
thousands of stone loaves splintering sunlight
their chiseled dates spanning a century
influenza   polio   HIV
lynchings   world wars   the sputtering
progress of democracy—
                        your true names waver
like heat thumbing asphalt   like history

the lives of others . . .
           Eunice   Clara   Mae
who charged with rage these out-of-fashion names
your Brookes and Chelseas candle in sleek throats
to mouth and summon if ever they pray
Prudence   Vera   Faith
            and you:
                Dorothy

dementia dawn

"lighght"
　　　　　　—Aram Saroyan

pokes all buttons　　on the bedside clock
till time grown ill　　no longer blinks

stillborn a.m.　　sponge-bathes for breakfast
silence　　tongues the narrow hall

no clatter　　no scrambled　　no low hubbub
where are the women　　who mirror her face

aides sway the confused　　bruised bone of her
back to her starlit room　　wrinkled bed

she lies　　one shoe off　　sweater wrongbuttoned
mind awash　　with the glimpse　　of clean

tablecloths　　unstained　　napkins　　unsoiled
plates　　such whiteness　　ringed with silver

awaiting the arrival　　of this day
that day　　this day

domestic disturbance

I'm calling the police   she'd shriek
before my father   gentled the phone from her fist

I'll break every dish in this house   she'd howl
shards pinwheeling   hardwood floors

face slapper   spitball of spite
crying out at night   *you never touch me*

why didn't my father   pillow her mouth
burn down the house   Chevrolet us away

how it wounds her   now   to revive the past
mom   I prod   what else have you lost

ashkenazi

---

who converted   after her sozzled
mother-in-law-to-be

banshee'd   at the bridal   shower
her altar boy   marrying a jew

who dutifully   each week
turned over   her thin paycheck

who stitched into satin
feathers & fleece

rows of young women
abuzz   in ivory   fluff

post-WWII   factory
National Powder Puff

white flight

& Sons   buys one brownstone
flips it   "blockbusting"   to a black family

there goes . . .   time to mobile up
time to flee   Brooklyn → Queens

Middle Village   lego'd on drained swampland
bounded by four   sprawling cemeteries

& Sons swears   black people afraid
always whistling   to walk among ghosts

mother wept   to leave   new neighbors
frontiered   next door

all of us   unseen   together
one family   sundialed in the riotous   garden

daughters taught me   the Wah-Watusi
son   the left jab   *sting like a bee*

wept   but never furnished
(they knew not to ask)   our new address

it wounds her   now   to relive the past
rageful   I press   who else have you lost

minecraft

---

mother in dementia   crying into the wilderness
into the imponderable   coils of the landline
too upset   to say why she's calling
just tell him   a voice insists

her grandson is missing   no one can find him
the residents   the staff
have scavenged each bathroom   storage closet
the parking lot   of her memory care facility

mom   I say   he's here   but don't tell her
he's building pyramids
block x block   secret chambers
labyrinths   impossible to negotiate

thank god she sobs   collapsing in relief

next visit   I ask   wasn't everyone angry
wheelchairs   gridlocked   in corridors
his name   hawked   into tumblers

no   she says   what's wrong with you
we were all so happy   we found him

sequins

---

grandmother Clara   lost both eyes
sewing sequins   onto mom's   hand-knit drab

first the mechanical   *click click*   of needles
then the silent   single needle   looping thread

millions of sequins   prisming my mother
in dresses of light   during WWII

then folded & stored   in a cedar chest
girlhood gone   the millions dead

those tinselly rags   exhumed by my nephew
retro rage   for the gay pride   parade

lip-syncing drag queen   *I Will Survive*
dazzling her darlings   their disco ball   alive

thanksgiving

---

after father passed   mom still prepared
our traditional dinner   butterball turkey

chunky gravy   walnut stuffing
creamed peas & onions   jellied cranberries

carved the bird   window'd the wishbone
simmered soup   from skeleton   then

tinfoil'd each slice   of succulent breast
strings of dark meat   drumsticks   wings

all the trimmings   spooned   into tupperware
froze the whole   fucking meal   each June

mom snowbirds   a few winters   in Florida
then buys a condo   next door   to her sister's

each morning   they raise the blinds   announcing
still alive   the blank page of sleep   erased

sisters ready   to begin again   the given day
until   sister'd out   they argue   stop talking

stop speaking   the language of blinds
dead or alive   no longer   anyone's concern

though days later   a visitor   knowing their routine
beholds both blinds   down   & not wanting

to discover   two corpses   phones the police
chastened   the sisters agree   no more silences

no more silences   mom clarifies   between condos

primer

---

is that my name   mom asks   slug scrawl
vaseline cursive   across garden paths

is that my name   she questions   squinting into sky
vapor trails   scored by jets   unbraiding

is *that* my name   Arabic script   storefront window
no   mom   that's not your name

taps my wrist   psss   someone's looking for me
searching America   my name   everywhere

and you   poet   didn't you ever learn   to read

twenty questions

---

what's that noise?
our neighbor's lawnmower

what's that noise?
someone's dog barking

what's that noise?
icemaker in the fridge

what's that noise?
Metallica

what's that noise?
mom   why do you keep asking?

Alice back from the hospital
heard the chariot coming

comin' for to carry her home?
this isn't a joke

the chariot full of angels
not choiring   exactly

said it was less music
than a rattling   like a spoon

stuck in the garbage disposal
or quarters in the dryer

like wheels needing grease
or the angels coughing

heard them under   the anesthesia
Alice knows   what she heard

what's that noise?
must be them angels

always the funny man
be quiet   help me listen

they could be coming for you

grocery list

Twizzlers   red   Orbit   spearmint
tea   Sleepy Time   Gypsy Cold Care

12 oz   12 pack   Poland Spring
to stave off   dehydration

each item   carefully penciled
but not one   chewed   steeped   swallowed

gum sticks   disappear   down glacial fissures
of tissue wads   whiting out   mom's pocketbook

tea tins   like flowerpots   brighten windowsills
Twizzlers stiffen   mass grave   in the bottom bin

plastic bottles   abide in rows   like processions
of schoolgirls   bearing votive   candles

St Cecilia   St Agnes   St Teresa of Avila
lighting the refrigerator   whenever   the door opens

staff

---

housekeeper   hides slippers   whammies clock

dining room servers   chitchat   indecipherably
clatter cups   inside her ear   scatter silverware

mom won't even   attempt   their names
Tawfiiq   Cabdulmajiid   Reinildis

letters scrambled   unpronounceable
complains   when they smile   *good mornin' Dot*

no respect   mom gripes
from Somali sons   Dominican daughters

always her girlname   never   Mrs Waters

game room

---

mom   plays bingo   dawn till dusk
full card   four corners   around the block
unless the caller   steals her dimes

fellow gamers   mom claims   whisper her name
avoid her glare   gather without her   even you
mom seethes   even you   won't hug me

bingo   twice yells   the milk-eyed granny

dimes

I bring mom   twenty dollars   bingo money
four rolls   200 dimes   wrapped tightly

we empty   each paper tube   onto a dish
swirl dimes   with fingertips

one dime   the Winged Liberty Head
minted   1916–1945

bears the image   of Elsie Moll
wife of the poet   Wallace Stevens

Mrs Stevens and I   went out
for a walk   yesterday afternoon

we walked   to the end   of Westerly Terrace
and she turned left   and I turned right

that's some coin   mom agrees
a whole marriage   trapped   in one thin dime

R

---

mom insists   she's no prude
but some films   screened after dinner

disgust her   whenever   the starlet's nude
she huffs out   with sister seniors

returns   to the tiny   Sony in her bedroom
views hoarders   survivors   short-fused chefs

unwilling to behold   Sally Hawkins'   breasts
Jennifer Lawrence's   breasts

recalling tonight   her own   lost ladies
that black & white   1947   movie

in which her groom   naked   gazed
upon her body   & didn't she

didn't she   gaze back

reality show

---

some folks   makeover   ramshackle vics
eyesores   transform into   Danube palaces

uncover Chagalls   in storage   garages
sew gowns   from garbage   for Heidi Klum

one moron   naked   in Peruvian jungle
gets stung   on the dick   by a wasp   mom laughs

that straight guy   given the queer eye
even he can see   these actors   don't fool anyone

you want reality   remember Alice?
stick around   for the memorial   service

crooner

Mel Tormé's   exhumed
for Sunday   afternoon   soirées

mom stammers along   as ribbons of song
unfray   throughout her brain

& shams a swoon   as this fat & bald &
black   jukebox

works the room   eager to please
wanting to be   velvet fog   for transported

ladies & three   last week four   Korean War
vets who   like poppies   clumped near the door

sleep through   mom's   routine request
Don't Get Around Much Anymore

sundowning

---

mom combs her hair   with a fork
silver tines catching   white knots

thumbs eyeglass case   to switch on Fox
undresses   dresses   undresses

one evening twice   calls me Ray
long gone husband   sad mistake

until in the window   I see
dead father   gasping back at me

family

_____

soup   tepid   teacup   unsaucer'd
tapioca   aquiver   in its chipped bowl

so when the harried   Haitian trainee
in response to a welcome   query

pauses to scroll   weekend selfies
as daughter-in-law   mother   serene wife

mom   unhinged   upbraids the woman
brandishing   her unclean   butter knife

criminal

---

because I will claim her   7:00 a.m.
for the psychiatric   evaluation

mom sleeps   in her red tracksuit
mouth lipstick'd   left arm hooked

through the pocketbook   strap
afraid to miss   the mandatory

monthly session   afraid to face
eviction   from her memory

care facility   she must have killed
someone   can't remember   who

whose bingo card   undimed
whose meds   still hidden   in applesauce

oh Dot   the lunch aide   lilts
you were missing   at breakfast

I know   mom nods   I murdered myself

meds

---

hearing aids   hazardous
pry one   apart

swallow   the battery
glittery pill   for her heart

icon

---

when you tumble   in the shower
I rush right over   & praise Whomever

no bones broken   only shaken   & you
shrunken   in your blue   bathrobe

aides & nurses   wandering off
to never-ending   dismal   duties

neighbors too   to rehearse   routine
unlovely   idiosyncrasies

slumped on the couch   you   lean against me
then slowly   unfold   the crumpled

parchment of your body   to lie across my lap
if anyone   returns   they'll see

living sculpture   almost familiar
son & mother   perverse Pietà

aura

---

*"The silken hair, too, had been suffered to grow all unheeded . . .
it floated rather than fell about the face . . ."*

      —Poe, "The Fall of the House of Usher"

I'm not at ease among mumbling geezers
who dodder past wheeling fist-gripped walkers

each a specter in a funhouse mirror
midway glimpse into pure erasure

until my dementia'd mother appears
& I fondle her unpinned ethereal hair

avian elegy

---

then my mother   grew smaller
the length of a wooden clothespin

wrapped in tissue   she lay
upon the birdcage floor
surrounded by seeds

someone had stolen the birdbath from our yard
wrested the concrete basin from its pillar
the pillar from the kingdom of earthworms

my mother had nowhere to go   no
rainwater to slake her thirst   to absolve her
I wore her feathered cloche   surrendered
to the silence   stunning the trees

I'm turning the mirror   mother
I'm turning the mirror

RED-BILLED FIREFINCH

Lagonosticta senegala

*"Birds called pithis, sold . . . across Senegal for a dime
. . . are believed to carry away sins when set free."*
—*The New York Times*

I whisper sins into empty birds,
Then set them free. So many sins, pithis
Untold. I watch them wing the sins away.

I buy finches from vendors in makeshift stalls,
Exotics in cages like sins in souls,
Touch lips to plumage where ears must be,

Then flick my finger to let loose each bird.
Have you heard my sins, scarlet flocks wheeling,
Unbound from my body? Have you witnessed

Modest comets arcing trees, feathery
Fireballs of forgiveness, plump pithis
Looping back now to hook claws within me?

LUKE 23:41

Asbury Park / Ocean Grove NJ

After hours, both signs read *Lifeguards Off Duty*,
But one beach insists *No Swimming*
While the other shrugs *Swim at Your Own Risk*.
That beach flaunts three tall crosses upright in sand.
Last summer I watched two dolphins
Arc lazily past one beach toward the other
While lifeguards whistled swimmers from the water.
One great brown triangular fin trailed those dolphins
Who swam at their own risk
Beyond crosses tossing shadows on bathers.
Where I swim I choose shark, preferring
The geometries of this world
To the wavering shadows of the next.
Let salt winnow what is false in me
Where creatures cruise dim shallows.
Let me test my luck
Outside the gloom of wood
On which one impenitent thief mocked salvation
While the other swerved
In the wisdom of suffering and understood
We are punished justly,
For we receive what our deeds deserve.

ELECTRIC FENCE

for my son, 10
in the first year of the presidency of Donald Trump

He dared me to touch my finger to the fence,
The fence which we'd been warned against.
Its wire whining mutely sparked my fingertip.
And he recalled the science teacher's lesson
About current and conduction, so
Grasped my hand and squinched his lids
As I prodded the wire once more.
We yelped as the splinter of lightning
Tore through my limbs into his.
Four cows, eyeing us, drooled deep indifference.
Next he coaxed his reluctant mom
To affix herself to this human chain . . .
Now the electricity needled us,
Stitching red thread through all three of us,
And could have leapt cross-country
Citizen to citizen unstoppably,
But instead fused fast the DNA
Of our stricken—and still smoldering—family.

THE WALL

1: Jerez de la Frontera

The bullet holes in the cathedral wall
Assume, like constellations, figurative
Poses—contorted corpses, limbs askew—
Though, oddly, most pockmarks & gouges
Flare darkly above our guide's Yankees cap.
We squint in the courtyard, looking up.
Farmers conscripted into firing squads
To execute cousins during '30s unrest
Waited until the final moment
To jerk their rifles slightly skyward.
Others aimed, too afraid
Under the watchful eyes of soldiers.
Even so, some mercifully missed. My son
Jabs a finger into each hole within reach.
He touches history, its evidence of death,
Its language of bullet & bayonet.

2: NYC

It was language that startled me
In the Broadway production of *King Lear*—
Edgar disguised as Poor Tom,
Hair all elf'd in knots,
Jabbering Spanish in counterfeit madness.
Theatergoers chuckled at the anti-Trumpian
Reference, one more less-than-subtle
& political directorial gesture—
Lear & Gloucester women, Albany
Black, Cornwall deaf & shadowed by his signer.
Diversity arced its rainbow flashings.
And the octogenarian actress as Lear,
Too frail to carry the dead daughter onstage,
Trundled funereally to her mark
As a trapdoor among the high catwalks
Sprung open & Cordelia descended,
Dangling from the hangman's noose.
We looked upward, my boy pointing,
His fingertip in the half-dark
Orchestra of the theater
Ghosted with the grit of a wall,
& "O, O, O, O," Lear moaned, then died
Suffering from such immeasurable sorrow, O
The cruelty & injustice of us all.

AMERICAN PASTORAL

"Pesticide exposure is attributed to higher rates of birth defects, developmental delays, leukemia, and brain cancer among farmworker children . . . the close proximity of agricultural fields to residential areas results in aerial drift of pesticides. . . ."

—*Farmworker Justice*

Sharp spice of fresh-cut lawn.
Clatter & drone
Of the neighbor's riding mower.
In my bed I dream *green*—
Green spatter on the visual
Artist's jeans, her canvas speckled
With grass & upon the grass a woman
Wearing a yellow apron
Raises a wooden clothespin
To pinch up rumpled squares
Of cobalt blue bedsheets
& between
Their wet almost blinding sheen
Like a march of imprinted baby ducks
Hangs a row of tiny socks
Belonging to the unseen
Toddler who grasps
The solace of color, the consolations
Of green, but not yet
The word or the sin or the murder
Descending upon grass
& brush-stroked
Within.

ONE CAW

Against the snow they're silhouettes,
These crows, how many hundreds
Burdening branches, these
Blunt-scissors-&-construction-paper
Kindergarten cut-outs, these
Rorschach blots, sloppy calligraphy,
Or jagged wounds, the sky torn,
But not political, if that's possible.
Then a blast scatters the murder
& any direction they flee is wrong.
Smoke on the hillside. The soldier
Stares, rifle tensed on one shoulder.
He's looking me over, wondering who I am.
I've seen this scene in films, Russian novels,
Old Master oils, Pathé newsreels.
Or on CNN—smoke in the city,
Schoolchildren scattered among rubble—
If that's possible—or blue sky, shade trees,
Suburban sprawl. The police car stops.
The boy stares. How many hundreds.
One caw, then silence.
Something horrible about to happen.

AOKIGAHARA

That forest in Japan where men noose themselves,
The mushrooms white with witness,
Where women slipper between trees,
Seduced by whispers they will soon become—

I would enter that forest to scoop one fistful
Of black soil from the needled floor,
To cull mushrooms safe enough for soup,
To recite aloud the names of loved ones

So those trees might know them
And seep their names to other forests
Along tunnels drilled through bone-dense dark
Root   by root   by root.

SONG OF ABSENCE

Because I've gone away from you

Longing branches my body
I take pleasure
In the softest tissue

Then sadness fills the room
Like smoke from the wick
Of a snuffed candle

Outside morning stars fizzle
The sky shuts its white door
Treetops turn invisible

The silk sheets of spiders
Once taut on tips of grass
Slump with dew

Because I've gone away from you

GOOD DEAD PERSON

Please don't inscribe my name on a tombstone,
Or place there a passage from my favorite book.
I have no favorite book.

Please don't chisel dates on my . . .
Please don't buy me a tombstone.

Please don't plant flowers on my grave.
I have no favorite flower.
I have allergies.

Please don't visit when the leaves redden,
Or snow whirls, or crocuses lift their purple cups.

Please don't circle the date on the calendar
To mark the anniversary of my death.
Don't say, "Six years gone," or "Twelve years gone."

When our children mention my name,
Insist that you don't remember me.

Tell them you remember nothing but my love,
Always there like the moon
Over Malta, Romania, the Dominican Republic.

ASHES

Maybe you'll ask our son to scatter
A few ounces of your ashes
Near the Ukrainian border
Where the body of the unknown saint
Unearthed by monks hunting mushrooms
Almost two centuries ago
Refuses to shed its fragrant flesh
Which assumes the spongy
Texture of tallow.
A young girl hiking countryside
During the communist regime,
You cradled the obscene head
And kissed those yellow lips,
Then ate a meal of soup and bread
Hunched alone at a rough-hewn table.
Despite that gesture of devotion,
The monastery will never claim
Fragments of your female frame.
Some believers have wealth enough
To satellite ashes into space,
Nearer My God to Thee,
Though that would be a waste of money.
One ambitious entrepreneur
Presses ashes into CDs
Which preserve the voice of the deceased,
So you could leave a farewell sound
Ghosting within
That round & impossibly thin
Unfashionable mausoleum.
                              Or
You might task our son with travel

To sow your ashes among the snowdrops
(Snowdrops always your favorite flower)
Lighting cemeteries near your home
Not far from the Ukrainian border.

for Mihaela

POSTSCRIPT TO *ASHES*

The small heap of *my* ashes, love, will be
Sieved into an anatomically
Precise, life-sized (sorry) rubber dildo

Which you should wield dexterously
To pleasure yourself while thinking of me
Watching you through the peephole of my halo.

CAPTAINS COURAGEOUS
BY RUDYARD KIPLING (1897)

"captains courageous, whom death could not daunt"
—anonymous ballad
Reliques of Ancient English Poetry (1765)

Thank you for the leather and wool watch cap
And for the silver ring watch, both

Linked by that word, *watch*,
As if they have something in common

Beyond their one-size-fits-all-ness
And their soon-to-be familiarity

With the underpinnings of my body,
One with the skull and one

With the right index finger bone,
So you too are linked with them,

Knowing my body better than anyone
As you keep watch over its slow

Disintegration, its crumbling vertebrae
And fissuring hernias, its left ear

Losing frequencies, its torn Achilles heel.
Thank you for these gifts to celebrate

My birthday, the serendipity
Of attaining the age of my father

When he died suddenly.
I'll lean into the indecipherable

Future as the seaman in his watch cap
Stands alone on deck at night,

Attempting to read the wind,
The minute shifts of weather, checking

His pocket watch once or twice to see
How many hours remain

Until his own shift ends, when he will
Toss his lit cigarette into the sea

And shamble off to bed where I will find you
Sleeping, the 19th-century novel splayed

Open on the comforter, the lamp still burning.

NOBODY'S POEM

In the solitude of this cottage room
Where the only sound is the on-again
Sotto voce whisper of the furnace
And the pipes' insistent knocking
As if the unwanted babe of the Muse,
Mewling creature swaddled in newspaper,
Has been dumped once more on the doorstep,
The floor-to-ceiling bookcase hoarding one wall
Filled with forty-year-old literary journals
Holds its breath.
                  If I move, if the air stirs,
The dust spouts again the words of poets
Listed in ten thousand Tables of Contents.
Even the journal in which this poem appears
Will be wedged in a wall among its brethren
Until someone down the decades draws it down
To drag one finger down the list of contributors:
Nobody, nobody, nobody, name, nobody, nobody
All the way down to the cold damp ground.

NOTES

The epigraphs to this collection are from "Crude Lament" by William Carlos Williams, *The Collected Poems Volume I: 1909–1939* (New Directions, 1986) and "Kaddish" by Allen Ginsberg, *Collected Poems 1947–1980* (Harper & Row, 1984).

"American Pastoral": epigraph: www.farmworkerjustice.org.

"Aokigahara": known as the Sea of Trees, this forest at the base of Mt. Fuji in Japan is morbidly famous for the hundreds of suicides that have taken place there.

"Bohemians": epigraph: "Introduction" by Karen Karbiener, *Leaves of Grass* by Walt Whitman (Barnes & Noble, 2005). Whitman uses the phrase "darlings and gossips" in a letter to Nat and Fred Gray dated March 19, 1863.

"crooner": in memory of Cliff Tyler (1932–2018)

"Dearest Creature": Sy Montgomery in *The Soul of an Octopus* (Atria Books, 2015) describes several incidents that triggered this poem.

"dementia dawn": epigraph: this one-word poem is included in *Complete Minimal Poems* by Aram Saroyan (Ugly Duckling Presse, 2007).

"dimes": Elsie Viola Kachel Moll (1886–1963) posed for sculptor Adolph A. Weinman for the image that appears on the Winged Liberty Head dime (often called, erroneously, the Mercury dime). Stevens is quoted in *Parts of a World: Wallace Stevens Remembered* by Peter Brazeau (Random House, 1983).

"Luke 23:41": for Laura McCullough. Ocean Grove, founded by Methodist clergymen in 1869, once known as the Queen of Religious

Resorts, now calls itself God's Square Mile. It remains a dry town, and its beach remains restricted on Sunday mornings.

"minecraft": the name of the popular video game released in 2009.

"Pileta Cave": Cueva de la Pileta (Cave of the Pool) is outside the town of Benaoján in the province of Málaga, Spain. I visited the cave in 2013. Vulvae are often depicted in rock art, even in that of "the most isolated inhabited place in the world": Easter Island. In 1770, claiming the island for Carlos III, "the Spanish commander, Felipe González de Haedo, asked the island chiefs to put their mark on a document of cession . . . [t]he Rapanui chiefs signed the document as best they could, with sketches of vulvas and frigate birds, signs familiar from the island's abundant rock art."—Jacob Mikanowski, "Language at the End of the World," *Cabinet* 64 (Summer 2017).

"R": the poem references indirectly the films *The Shape of Water* (2017) and *Red Sparrow* (2018), respectively. My parents married on August 3, 1947.

"Red-Billed Firefinch": epigraph: "Absolution, With a Wing and a Prayer" by Jaime Yaya Barry, *The New York Times*, October 5, 2016. These finches are also known as "birds of forgiveness."

"*Self-Portrait with Doll* (1920–21)": the title of a painting by Oskar Kokoschka. There are accounts of this doll online and in print, including one in Robert Hughes' *Nothing If Not Critical* (Penguin, 1992). Several online accounts display photographs of the doll.

"Swyve": although some scholars translate "swyve" as "screw," others, including the unacknowledged translator on librarius.com ("As, if I can, that very wench I'll fuck") and, more recently, Peter Ackroyd ("I am goin' to fuck their daughter") in his "retelling" of *The Canterbury Tales* (Penguin, 2009), prefer the more vulgar version.

"twenty questions": references the African-American spiritual "Swing Low, Sweet Chariot" and 2 Kings 2:11 upon which it is based.

"Vs.": "heart's needle": the title poem of a book (1959) by W. D. Snodgrass, who took the phrase from a medieval Irish tale, *Buile Suibhne* ("The Frenzy of Suibne"), translated by Myles Dillon in 1948. More recently, the tale was translated by Seamus Heaney as *Sweeney Astray* (1983).

"The Wall": the 2019 Broadway production of *King Lear* starred Glenda Jackson.

ACKNOWLEDGMENTS

Warm thanks for their generous support to the editors and staffs of the journals and books in which these poems, sometimes in earlier versions, appeared:

The American Poetry Review: "the book of names";
The Anglican Theological Review: "Aokigahara";
Gargoyle: "Spelling Lesson";
The Georgia Review: "Dearest Creature," "Red-Billed Firefinch";
The Gettysburg Review: "avian elegy," "minecraft," "One Last Beat," Swyve";
Great River Review: "Ashes," "Bohemians," "*Captains Courageous* by Rudyard Kipling (1897)," "Postscript to *Ashes*," "*Self-Portrait with Doll* (1920–21)";
The Hopkins Review: "Good Riddance Chicken," "Luke 23:41";
ISLE: Interdisciplinary Studies in Literature and Environment: "American Pastoral";
J Journal: New Writing on Justice: "Electric Fence";
The Kipling Journal (UK): "*Captains Courageous* by Rudyard Kipling (1897)";
New Letters: "Good Dead Person," "Sherry," "Vs.";
Plume: "The Wall";
The Progressive: "One Caw";
Redactions: Poetry & Poetics: "dimes," "icon," "sequins";
Solstice: "Nobody's Poem";
Southern Indiana Review: "domestic disturbance," "primer," "sundowning," "white flight";
Spillway: "Pileta Cave";
This Broken Shore: "Song of Absence."

"the book of names" appeared in *Celestial Joyride* (BOA Editions, 2016).

"Scientific American" and "Song of Absence" appeared in *Like Light: 25 Years of Poetry and Prose*, ed. Bertha Rogers (Bright Hill Press, 2017).

"avian elegy" and "Good Dead Person," translated by Frances Simán, appeared in the journal *Hablemos Claro* (June 2019) in Honduras.

"Good Dead Person" was made into an animated short film by Gal Cohen and Shany Nisim of the Minshar School of Art in Israel under the auspices of Moving Words 2019/ARTS by the People with the support of The Santiago Abut Foundation. Special thanks to David Crews.

"One Caw" & "*Self-Portrait with Doll* (1920–21)" were reprinted in *Across the Waves: Contemporary Poetry from Ireland and the United States*, ed. Jean O'Brien & Gerry LaFemina (Salmon, 2020).

"Aokigahara" was reprinted in *Rewilding: Poems for the Environment*, ed. Crystal S. Gibbins (Flexible Press, 2020).

I remain grateful to the John Simon Guggenheim Memorial Foundation for a 2017 Fellowship, to the Virginia Center for the Creative Arts for residency fellowships in 2017 and 2018 . . .

to colleagues at Monmouth University: Mary Kate Azcuy, Melissa Febos, Alex Gilvarry, Susan Goulding, Alena Graedon, Laura Moriarty, Michael Paul Thomas, and Kenneth Womack . . .

to colleagues in the Drew University MFA Program in Poetry and Poetry in Translation: Sean Nevin, Alicia Ostriker, Sarah Vap, Ellen Doré Watson, Afaa Michael Weaver and, especially, Judith Vollmer for her keen (and crucial) attention to the making of this book . . .

to Ed Ochester, Sheila Pleasants, and Harold Schechter for various kindnesses . . .

to the generous and meticulous staff at BOA: Peter Conners, Kelly Hatton, Ron Martin-Dent, and Daphne Morrissey . . .

and to Mihaela Moscaliuc, *iubita mea*, for helping me attempt to get it all right, here and everywhere else.

In memory of Kathleen Sheeder Bonanno (1955–2017)
and David Bonnano (1949–2017).

ABOUT THE AUTHOR

Michael Waters is the recipient of fellowships from the Guggenheim Foundation, National Endowment for the Arts, Fulbright Foundation, and New Jersey State Council on the Arts. He lives without a cell phone in Ocean, New Jersey.

BOA EDITIONS, LTD.
AMERICAN POETS CONTINUUM SERIES

COLOPHON

BOA Editions, Ltd., a not-for-profit publisher of poetry and other literary works, fosters readership and appreciation of contemporary literature. By identifying, cultivating, and publishing both new and established poets and selecting authors of unique literary talent, BOA brings high-quality literature to the public.

Support for this effort comes from the sale of its publications, grant funding, and private donations.

The publication of this book is made possible, in part, by the special support of the following individuals:

Anonymous
Susan DeWitt Davie
Richard Foerster
David Fraher, *in memory of A. Poulin, Jr.*
James Long Hale
Melissa Hall & Joe Torre
Sandi Henschel, *in memory of Anthony Piccione*
Barbara & John Lovenheim
Joe McElveney
Dan Meyers, *in honor of J. Shepard Skiff*
Dorrie Parini & Paul LaFerriere
Boo Poulin
Steven O. Russell & Phyllis Rifkin-Russell
Allan & Melanie Ulrich
William Waddell & Linda Rubel